E PLURIBUS UNUM

BY THE PEOPLE

THE U.S. PRESIDENCY

Bill McAuliffe

Creative Education ★ Creative Paperbacks

TABLE OF CONTENTS

★ ★ ★

George Washington said that when he became the first president of the United States, he felt like "a culprit who is going to his place of execution."

THE U.S. PRESIDENCY

On leaving office, Thomas Jefferson said, "Never did a prisoner, released from his chains, feel such relief as I shall on shaking off the shackles of power." Today, a president never drives his own car. His kids must have people guarding them in school. He can't even get a pay raise. Who'd want a job like that? Many people. And they organize thousands of workers and raise millions of dollars to try to get elected. That's because the president has the power to make and change history. He—or she, if a woman ever gets elected—is one of the most influential people on Earth. The job, created by the people, is the only one in the world with the title "Leader of the Free World."

Washington was the unanimous choice of the electoral college for both of his terms.

PRESIDENTIAL CANDIDATE REQUIREMENTS

AS OUTLINED IN ARTICLE II OF THE CONSTITUTION

BE A NATURAL-BORN CITIZEN OF THE UNITED STATES

HAVE BEEN A RESIDENT OF THE UNITED STATES FOR THE PAST ★ 14 ★ YEARS

BE AT LEAST 35 YEARS OLD

CHAPTER 1

STILL A WORK IN PROGRESS

THE U.S. PRESIDENCY

Before 1787, no one had ever heard of a government being led by a president. Kings and queens were common around the world then. But the founders of the U.S. had just fought and won a war to escape the power of King George III of England. They thought he had used his powers unfairly, demanding taxes without their representation. They wanted to make their own laws. And they wanted a leader they would choose for themselves. It was a **radical** idea for its time.

When 39 leaders signed the Constitution, the document organizing the U.S. government, they didn't seem to know exactly what they wanted the head of the government to be, or even do. They started with the duties of Congress in Article I. But they didn't deal with the presidency until Article II. That suggests to some constitutional scholars that the founders were more

44th PRESIDENT BARACK OBAMA

★ In fact, all the Constitution requires is that the president must be at least 35 years old, be a natural-born U.S. citizen, and have lived in the U.S. for 14 years. ★

STILL A WORK IN PROGRESS

concerned about Congress than the presidency. Perhaps this was because Congress would be the branch of government closest to representing the citizens of the new nation.

Much of Article II deals with presidential election and **presidential succession**. It says very little about the president's actual duties and powers. Article II indicates that the president would: be the head of the army and navy (commander in chief); ask for reports from the heads of members of his **cabinet**; be able to pardon people who'd committed crimes against the U.S.; make treaties; nominate ambassadors, judges, and other public ministers; provide a regular State of the Union message; and

not get a pay raise once elected.

As for qualifications, the Constitution is silent about job experience or education. It doesn't say horse thieves and bank robbers can't become president. And there's no mention of parents, ancestors, or religion, which were common baselines for royal leadership in monarchies elsewhere. In fact, all the Constitution requires is that the president must be at least 35 years old, be a natural-born U.S. citizen, and have lived in the U.S. for 14 years.

That means millions of people in the U.S., then and now, are qualified to be president. But since the earliest days of the country, various cultural factors all but eliminated much of the population from

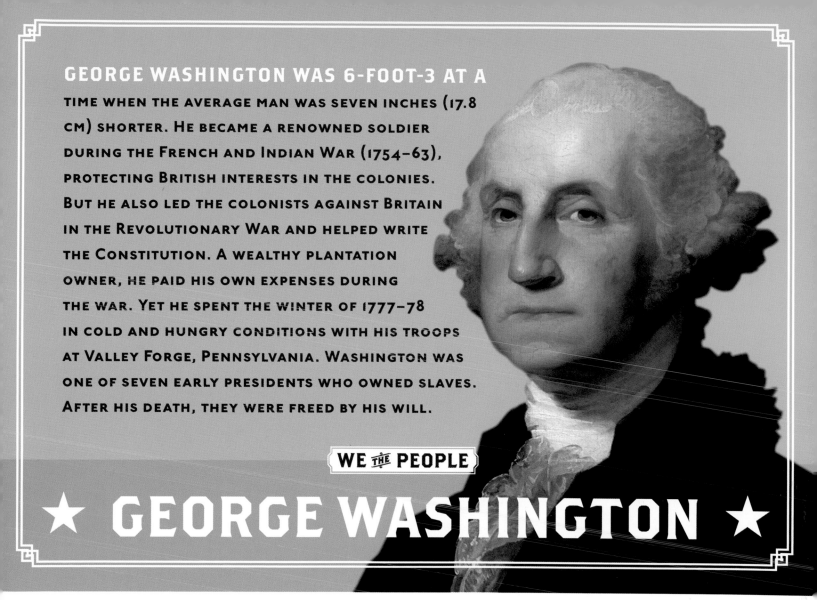

GEORGE WASHINGTON WAS 6-FOOT-3 AT A TIME WHEN THE AVERAGE MAN WAS SEVEN INCHES (17.8 CM) SHORTER. HE BECAME A RENOWNED SOLDIER DURING THE FRENCH AND INDIAN WAR (1754–63), PROTECTING BRITISH INTERESTS IN THE COLONIES. BUT HE ALSO LED THE COLONISTS AGAINST BRITAIN IN THE REVOLUTIONARY WAR AND HELPED WRITE THE CONSTITUTION. A WEALTHY PLANTATION OWNER, HE PAID HIS OWN EXPENSES DURING THE WAR. YET HE SPENT THE WINTER OF 1777–78 IN COLD AND HUNGRY CONDITIONS WITH HIS TROOPS AT VALLEY FORGE, PENNSYLVANIA. WASHINGTON WAS ONE OF SEVEN EARLY PRESIDENTS WHO OWNED SLAVES. AFTER HIS DEATH, THEY WERE FREED BY HIS WILL.

WE THE PEOPLE

★ GEORGE WASHINGTON ★

ever becoming president.

Consider that Barack Obama, elected to his first term in 2008, was the nation's first black president. Until the 13th **Amendment** to the Constitution was approved in 1865, the U.S. allowed slavery. Slavery essentially involved the treatment of some people as property and gave others the right to buy and sell them. The Constitution, in fact, reinforced slaves' inferior status. It denied them citizenship and counted each slave as three-fifths of a person. Even after slavery was outlawed, blacks were prevented from voting throughout much of the 19th and 20th centuries by literacy tests and taxes charged at polling places. "Jim Crow" laws in the South and other types of segregation in the North kept blacks from voting or running for office.

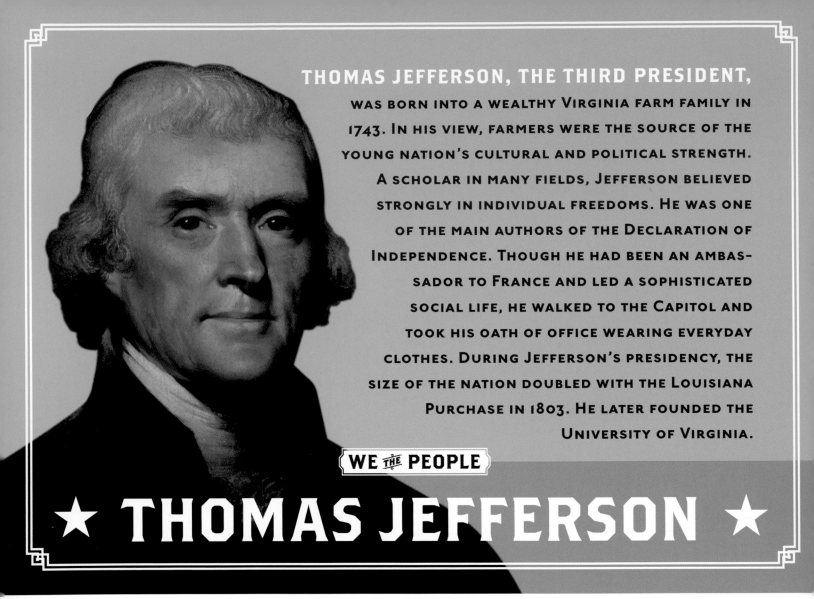

THOMAS JEFFERSON, THE THIRD PRESIDENT, WAS BORN INTO A WEALTHY VIRGINIA FARM FAMILY IN 1743. IN HIS VIEW, FARMERS WERE THE SOURCE OF THE YOUNG NATION'S CULTURAL AND POLITICAL STRENGTH. A SCHOLAR IN MANY FIELDS, JEFFERSON BELIEVED STRONGLY IN INDIVIDUAL FREEDOMS. HE WAS ONE OF THE MAIN AUTHORS OF THE DECLARATION OF INDEPENDENCE. THOUGH HE HAD BEEN AN AMBASSADOR TO FRANCE AND LED A SOPHISTICATED SOCIAL LIFE, HE WALKED TO THE CAPITOL AND TOOK HIS OATH OF OFFICE WEARING EVERYDAY CLOTHES. DURING JEFFERSON'S PRESIDENCY, THE SIZE OF THE NATION DOUBLED WITH THE LOUISIANA PURCHASE IN 1803. HE LATER FOUNDED THE UNIVERSITY OF VIRGINIA.

★ THOMAS JEFFERSON ★

Similarly, the nation has never elected a woman as president. The Constitution did not extend to women a uniform, national right to vote until the 19th Amendment was passed in 1920. Few women ran for office until recently, and they are still in the minority in most legislative bodies. Because that has limited their visibility in policymaking, it could be said that the presidency has traditionally been closed to women as well.

Most presidents, particularly early on, came from wealthy and influential families. But many, from George Washington (1789–97) to John F. Kennedy (1961–63), were notable war heroes, too. A typical path to the presidency involves serving as a senator, governor, or other elected official. A candidate might be extremely well-educated, be a successful manager, understand

the law and public policy, have experience in economics and finance, speak several languages, be a military veteran, and maybe even have been elected to office in some state. But unless he has nurtured a national reputation, he's simply not going to be seen as presidential material.

Before serving as a congressman or president, Kennedy was a gunboat pilot.

At first, Congress—not the president—was regarded as the center of political power. Scholars have described some of the presidents in the nation's first half-century as being able clerks, or record keepers. Over time, major historical crises have prompted dramatic expansions in the powers of both the president

★ **But presidents also wield a more personal type of power while in office. That is the power to connect with citizens almost as a neighbor.** ★

STILL A WORK IN PROGRESS

and the federal government. Abraham Lincoln (1861–65) profoundly increased presidential influence during the Civil War. Franklin D. Roosevelt (1933–45) took similar actions during the Great Depression and World War II. Both are known today as being among the most effective presidents in history.

But presidents also wield a more personal type of power while in office. That is the power to connect with citizens almost as a neighbor. Fifth president James Monroe (1817–25) established the value of public appearances, making

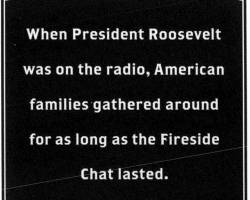

When President Roosevelt was on the radio, American families gathered around for as long as the Fireside Chat lasted.

tours of the growing nation a regular feature of his presidency. Theodore Roosevelt (1901–09) made sure reporters, photographers, and moviemakers helped him build his larger-than-life image as a rugged outdoorsman, war hero, boxer, big-game hunter, and world traveler. Decades later, Franklin D. Roosevelt used the radio to put himself in Americans' living rooms. His periodic "Fireside Chats" on policy and the events of World War II endeared him to citizens. Ever-intensifying news coverage has established a familiarity with the president and

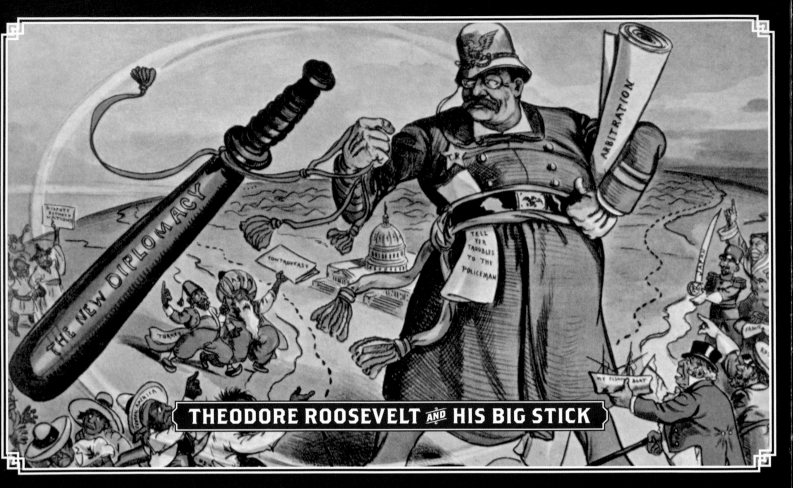

THEODORE ROOSEVELT AND HIS BIG STICK

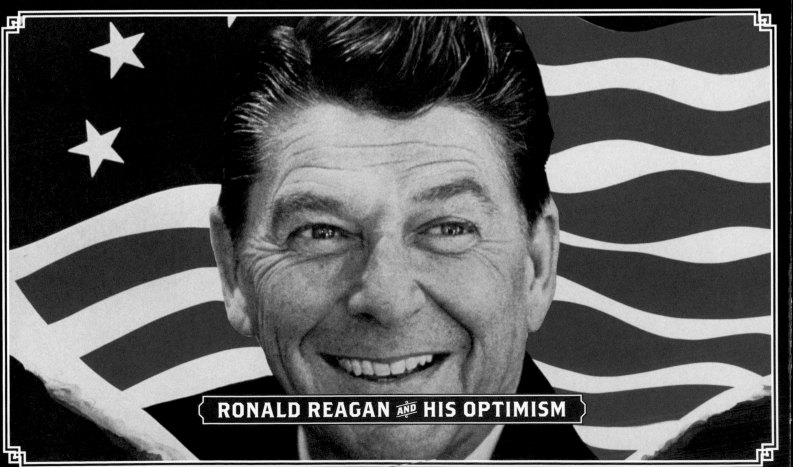

RONALD REAGAN AND HIS OPTIMISM

PARDONED TURKEY

STILL A WORK IN PROGRESS

his family that the Founding Fathers never could have envisioned. Today, it's possible for individuals to connect with President Obama on Twitter (@BarackObama).

Historians also often describe how the best-known presidents had personalities that reflected prevailing attitudes or pulled the nation's mood in a new direction. The dynamic Theodore Roosevelt said the country should "talk softly and carry a big stick." He rode that idea to tremendous popularity and established the U.S. as a

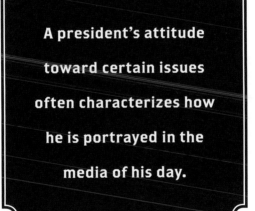

A president's attitude toward certain issues often characterizes how he is portrayed in the media of his day.

world leader. Seven decades later, Ronald Reagan (1981–89) was thought to embody a new optimism after the embattled presidency of Jimmy Carter (1977–81).

Presidents have also been known to have a little fun with their powers. For more than a century, they have marked Thanksgiving by granting a turkey a presidential pardon, sparing the turkey a death sentence. It's never earned any of them a vote, but it's kept them in front of the news cameras.

GEORGE WASHINGTON ⚔ THE WHISKEY REBELLION

WITH THE FEDERAL GOVERNMENT IN DEBT, CONGRESS PLACED A TAX ON LIQUOR IN 1791.

Throughout the western frontier, people distilled whiskey. The liquor was used as a form of currency, and it was easier to transport than the grain it was made from. When Congress passed a law taxing distilled liquor in 1791, the people rebelled. The greatest uproar came from western Pennsylvania, where tax collectors were attacked and frequently tarred and feathered (an old form of punishment). In 1794, **PRESIDENT GEORGE WASHINGTON** led about 13,000 troops to the epicenter of the Whiskey Rebellion in western Pennsylvania. After several arrests were made, the rebellion died down. All those arrested were later pardoned or found not guilty.

FEDERAL AUTHORITY TO ENFORCE TAXES WAS CHALLENGED FOR THE FIRST TIME.

☞ Washington ordered about 13,000 troops to western Pennsylvania to smother the rebellion.

CHAPTER 2

THE PEOPLE IN THE WHITE HOUSE

THE U.S. PRESIDENCY

Some would prefer that the president stick to the few duties outlined in Article II. But that job description doesn't say what the president *cannot* do. Presidents have steadily pushed against whatever boundaries were set, or not set, by the Constitution.

Washington had been a wealthy landowner, wilderness battle veteran, Revolutionary War commander, and shaper of the Constitution when he was elected president in 1789. He used his status to appear "above politics," focusing on stabilizing the new nation's finances. But while president he also rode into a battle against tax-resisting, wilderness whiskey-makers. Such action showed the federal government's readiness to enforce its own laws, even when people doubted the value of a central government.

★ His wartime executive order known as the Emancipation Proclamation freed slaves in the states rebelling against the Union. Lincoln described the act as a military strategy. ★

THE PEOPLE IN THE WHITE HOUSE

Similarly, seventh president Andrew Jackson (1829–37) used military force to collect federal **tariffs** in South Carolina. He also used the presidential power to **veto** laws more than any of his predecessors had. This revealed a significant ability unique to the president.

Later, Abraham Lincoln made special use of his authority as commander in chief during the Civil War. His wartime executive order known as the Emancipation Proclamation freed slaves in the states rebelling against the Union. Lincoln described the act as a military strategy. It was intended to sap the strength of the rebel states, where slaves were being used in businesses and activities supporting their war effort. Many freed slaves became

Union soldiers, which benefitted the North.

Proposing new laws was originally reserved for Congress. But today, even people running for president suggest detailed legislation or changes to existing laws. Once elected, a president often uses the annual State of the Union address to announce what policies he wants Congress to adopt.

In the 20th century, Franklin D. Roosevelt made the federal government an active force in the lives of everyday Americans. He started a wide range of employment programs and aid policies during the Great Depression. Among them were farm **subsidies** and the Social Security Act. These programs continue to provide income sources to farmers and elderly and disabled people. Ever since the

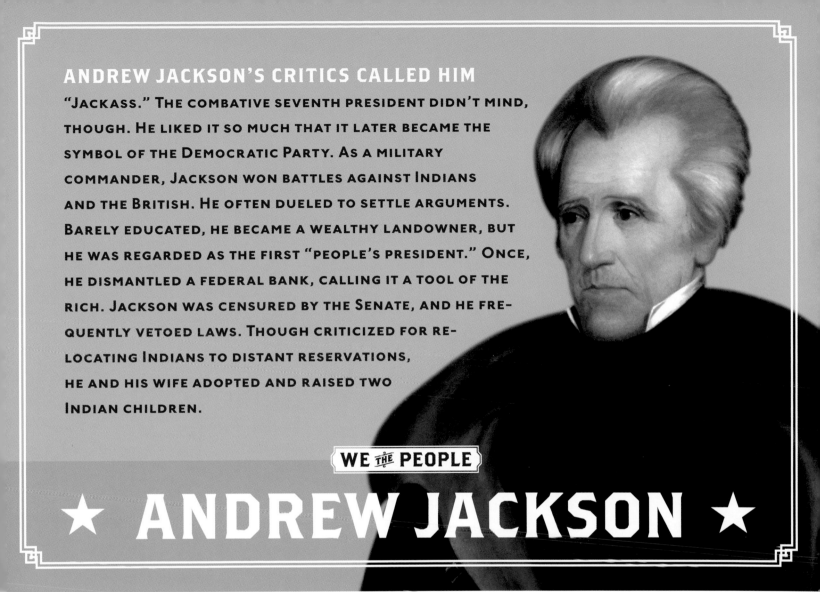

ANDREW JACKSON'S CRITICS CALLED HIM "JACKASS." THE COMBATIVE SEVENTH PRESIDENT DIDN'T MIND, THOUGH. HE LIKED IT SO MUCH THAT IT LATER BECAME THE SYMBOL OF THE DEMOCRATIC PARTY. AS A MILITARY COMMANDER, JACKSON WON BATTLES AGAINST INDIANS AND THE BRITISH. HE OFTEN DUELED TO SETTLE ARGUMENTS. BARELY EDUCATED, HE BECAME A WEALTHY LANDOWNER, BUT HE WAS REGARDED AS THE FIRST "PEOPLE'S PRESIDENT." ONCE, HE DISMANTLED A FEDERAL BANK, CALLING IT A TOOL OF THE RICH. JACKSON WAS CENSURED BY THE SENATE, AND HE FREQUENTLY VETOED LAWS. THOUGH CRITICIZED FOR RELOCATING INDIANS TO DISTANT RESERVATIONS, HE AND HIS WIFE ADOPTED AND RAISED TWO INDIAN CHILDREN.

WE THE PEOPLE

★ ANDREW JACKSON ★

1930s, citizens have expected more of the federal government.

The president does not have the authority to declare war. Only Congress can do that. (Congress has declared war only five times—and always at the urging of the president.) But as commanders in chief of the armed forces, presidents have repeatedly sent American troops into conflicts around the world. This usually has happened without a congressional declaration of war.

There is another way in which presidents can have influence that outlasts their time in office. That is through the appointment of judges, particularly those on the Supreme Court. Those nine judges settle disputes and decide the **constitutionality** of laws. Sometimes they deal with the most intense controversies of the day. But because Supreme Court justices have lifetime

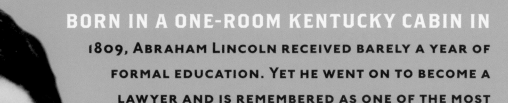

appointments, a president's power to shape the court and his own legacy is unpredictable. Washington was able to appoint more justices than any other president, 10. But four presidents, including Carter, appointed none.

Creating an office held by a single person who would balance power with Congress and the courts was certain to make that person a significant figure. The framers of the Constitution designed a curious process to ensure the president wouldn't owe his election to Congress or to a large-scale popular vote. Either scenario might have been easily corrupted, particularly in the nation's early days, when cross-country travel and communication were especially difficult.

The Constitution set forth that presidents would be chosen by electors, who themselves were chosen for that duty in each state (and, later, also in the District of Columbia). The

number of electors equaled the number of U.S. senators and representatives from each state. The electors would vote for two candidates, at least one of whom had to be from a different state. The electors' votes would then be counted by the Senate. The person with the most votes would be declared president. The person with the

second-most would be vice president. What could go wrong?

A lot. In 1796, John Adams and Thomas Jefferson finished first and second in the voting, making them president and vice president respectively. But they were political rivals—a recipe for **intrigue** and **stalemate** at the top

Before Article I is the famous preamble, or introduction, to the Constitution.

★ **In 2000, Democratic candidate Al Gore received the highest number of popular votes. However, after a messy attempt to recount votes in Florida and a decision by the Supreme Court, Republican George W. Bush won in the electoral college.** ★

THE PEOPLE IN THE WHITE HOUSE

of government. Four years later, Jefferson and Aaron Burr actually tied in the presidential election. That threw the decision to the House of Representatives. It took 36 ballots for Jefferson to gain a majority and win. Before the next election, in 1804, Congress passed and the states authorized the 12th Amendment. This declared that electors would vote for only one person for president and another for vice president.

Though Congress has tried to get rid of the electoral college and have the president chosen directly by the people, it's still

> When the Supreme Court stopped the Florida recount, Bush was ahead by 537 votes, which gave him the state's electoral vote.

electors who decide. In most cases, electors are pledged to vote in accordance with the popular vote in their state. But such an outcome can cause disputes. In 2000, Democratic candidate Al Gore received the highest number of popular votes. However, after a messy attempt to recount votes in Florida and a decision by the Supreme Court, Republican George W. Bush won in the electoral college. He had 271 votes, one more than the 270-vote majority required. Gore received 266. Bush became the 43rd president and served two terms.

Washington established the custom of

WHY DO
PRIVATE
COMPANIES
COUNT
PUBLIC
VOTES?
RECOUNT
RE-VOTE
OR
REVOLT

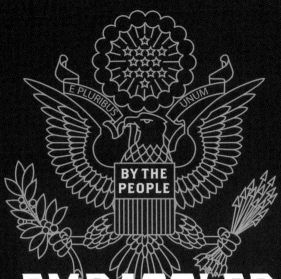

EMBATTLED PRESIDENTS

IMPEACHED

ANDREW JOHNSON was impeached by the House of Representatives in 1868 for violating the Tenure of Office Act. Passed in 1867, the act was meant to protect the secretary of war, Edwin M. Stanton. Johnson disregarded the act, fired Stanton, and replaced him with Ulysses S. Grant. The Senate vote failed by one to remove Johnson from office.

RESIGNED

RICHARD NIXON resigned amid scandal in 1974. By resigning, he avoided likely impeachment and removal from office. Nixon and members of his administration were discovered to have been complicit in a 1972 burglary at the Democratic National Committee headquarters.

IMPEACHED

BILL CLINTON was impeached in 1998 by the House of Representatives. The House charged Clinton with perjury and obstruction of justice during an investigation of his conduct and an extramarital affair. The Senate acquitted him in 1999.

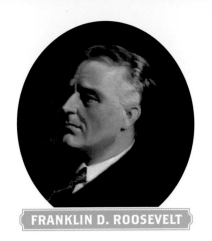

THE PEOPLE IN THE WHITE HOUSE

presidents serving two terms if they won reelection. However, the immensely popular Franklin D. Roosevelt broke that **precedent** by getting elected four times. Roosevelt, a Democrat, died early in his fourth term. Republicans won control of Congress two years later in 1947. They passed the 22nd Amendment (approved by the states in 1951), which limits a person to two elections as president. Of the 44 presidents through Obama, 16 were elected at least twice, including Grover Cleveland (1885–89, 1893–97), whose two terms were separated by the presidency of Benjamin Harrison (1889–93).

Unless a president becomes disabled in some way, the only way to have him removed from office is through **impeachment**. The House may impeach a president, the Constitution says, only if he's thought to have committed **treason**, **bribery**, or other "high crimes and Misdemeanors." The Senate then puts him on trial. Only two presidents— Andrew Johnson (1865–69) and Bill Clinton (1993–2001) have been impeached, although neither was removed from office. Richard Nixon (1969–74) remains the only president to ever resign his seat. He did so to avoid likely impeachment for numerous criminal acts surrounding his 1972 reelection campaign.

> Franklin Roosevelt became the seventh president to die while in office; before him was Warren Harding in 1923.

SECRETARY OF
DEFENSE

SECRETARY OF
HOMELAND SECURITY

SECRETARY OF
ENERGY

SECRETARY OF
EDUCATION

SECRETARY OF
TRANSPORTATION

VICE PRESIDENT

SECRETARY OF THE
INTERIOR

SECRETARY OF
AGRICULTURE

SECRETARY OF
HEALTH AND HUMAN SERVICES

SECRETARY OF
HOUSING AND URBAN DEVELOPMENT

SECRETARY OF
LABOR

SECRETARY OF
COMMERCE

SECRETARY OF THE
TREASURY

ATTORNEY GENERAL

SECRETARY OF
VETERANS AFFAIRS

SECRETARY OF
STATE

CHAPTER 3

UNCOVERING POWERS

THE U.S. PRESIDENCY

The president's responsibilities are far more extensive and detailed today than they were two centuries ago. When Washington was president, he met with a cabinet of four people—the secretaries of war, treasury, and state, and an attorney general. The Obama White House had a staff of more than 400 people. His cabinet included vice president Joe Biden, the attorney general, who is head of the Justice Department, and the heads of 14 other departments: Agriculture, Commerce, Defense, Education, Energy, Health and Human Services, Homeland Security, Housing and Urban Development, Interior, Labor, State, Transportation, Treasury, and Veterans Affairs. These federal executive departments, along with the rest of the White House staff, make up the executive branch of the government. This branch employs more than 2 million people. That's close to the entire population of the original 13 states!

VIETNAM CONFLICT

★ **Most of the military campaigns in which the U.S. has participated have not technically been wars.** ★

UNCOVERING POWERS

As far-reaching as the president's management is, chief executives continue to assert power in new ways. They jockey with Congress and the Supreme Court over the balance of power. Often, to justify actions or deal with unforeseen events, presidents will look for the blank spots in the Constitution—where many powers are not specifically prohibited.

For example, the Constitution allows "emergency powers" for a president to commit troops to battle in response to an attack on the U.S. Most of the military campaigns in which the U.S. has participated have not technically been wars. But some of them were commonly known as "wars" anyway: the Gulf War, the Iraq War, the Vietnam War, the Korean War, and even the Indian Wars carried out as American settlement expanded westward during the 19th century. All have featured some level of cooperation between the president and Congress, at the very least because Congress had to authorize money to pay for military expenses. The president's influence in such conflicts stems from his constitutionally defined role as commander in chief of the armed forces.

The nearly decade-long conflict in Vietnam, which at its height involved 500,000 American troops and saw more than 50,000 killed, went without strict congressional approval. It generated intense opposition in Congress and throughout

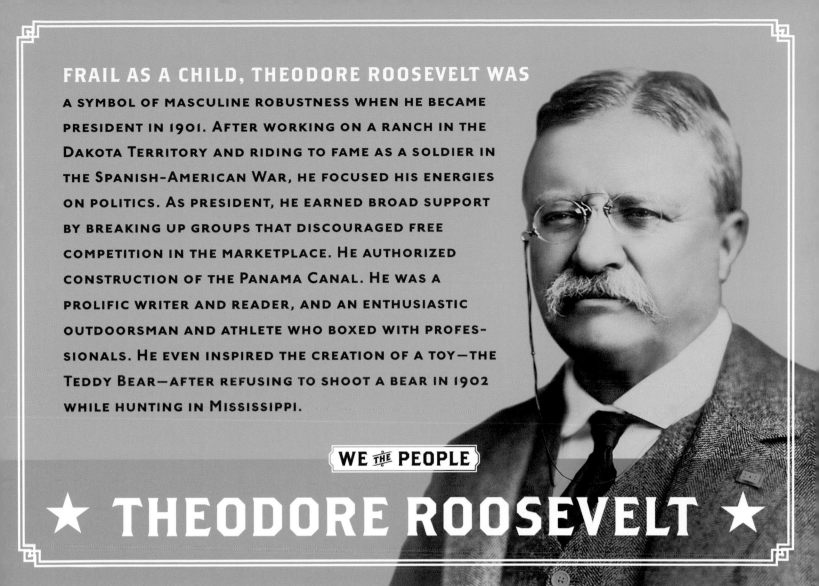

FRAIL AS A CHILD, THEODORE ROOSEVELT WAS A SYMBOL OF MASCULINE ROBUSTNESS WHEN HE BECAME PRESIDENT IN 1901. AFTER WORKING ON A RANCH IN THE DAKOTA TERRITORY AND RIDING TO FAME AS A SOLDIER IN THE SPANISH-AMERICAN WAR, HE FOCUSED HIS ENERGIES ON POLITICS. AS PRESIDENT, HE EARNED BROAD SUPPORT BY BREAKING UP GROUPS THAT DISCOURAGED FREE COMPETITION IN THE MARKETPLACE. HE AUTHORIZED CONSTRUCTION OF THE PANAMA CANAL. HE WAS A PROLIFIC WRITER AND READER, AND AN ENTHUSIASTIC OUTDOORSMAN AND ATHLETE WHO BOXED WITH PROFESSIONALS. HE EVEN INSPIRED THE CREATION OF A TOY—THE TEDDY BEAR—AFTER REFUSING TO SHOOT A BEAR IN 1902 WHILE HUNTING IN MISSISSIPPI.

WE THE PEOPLE

★ THEODORE ROOSEVELT ★

the rest of the country. It ultimately caused president Lyndon B. Johnson (1963–69) to not seek a second term. As U.S. involvement wound down, Congress passed the War Powers Resolution of 1973. This requires a president to tell Congress within 48 hours about any commitment of troops. It also calls for the president to remove all troops after 60 days, if Congress has not granted an extension.

Presidents have worked along the margins of that measure as well. Clinton's 1999 Kosovo bombing campaign was authorized by Congress but went beyond the War Powers Resolution's deadline for troop removal. George W. Bush (2001–09), in the Iraq War, was checked by the Supreme Court several times after he sent prisoners to Guantánamo Bay in Cuba. This prevented the detainees from claiming legal

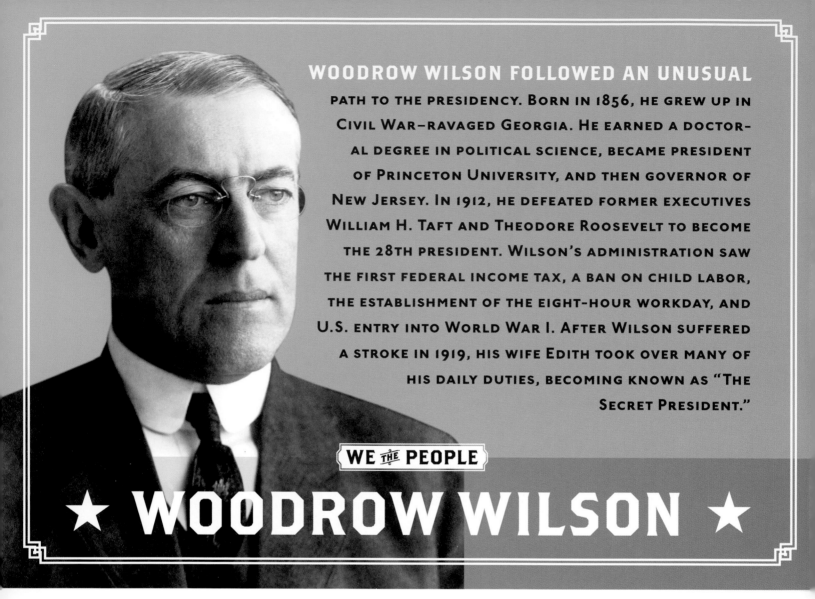

WOODROW WILSON FOLLOWED AN UNUSUAL PATH TO THE PRESIDENCY. BORN IN 1856, HE GREW UP IN CIVIL WAR–RAVAGED GEORGIA. HE EARNED A DOCTORAL DEGREE IN POLITICAL SCIENCE, BECAME PRESIDENT OF PRINCETON UNIVERSITY, AND THEN GOVERNOR OF NEW JERSEY. IN 1912, HE DEFEATED FORMER EXECUTIVES WILLIAM H. TAFT AND THEODORE ROOSEVELT TO BECOME THE 28TH PRESIDENT. WILSON'S ADMINISTRATION SAW THE FIRST FEDERAL INCOME TAX, A BAN ON CHILD LABOR, THE ESTABLISHMENT OF THE EIGHT-HOUR WORKDAY, AND U.S. ENTRY INTO WORLD WAR I. AFTER WILSON SUFFERED A STROKE IN 1919, HIS WIFE EDITH TOOK OVER MANY OF HIS DAILY DUTIES, BECOMING KNOWN AS "THE SECRET PRESIDENT."

WE THE PEOPLE

★ WOODROW WILSON ★

protection in the U.S.

During the Civil War, Lincoln suspended habeas corpus, one of the key individual liberties named in the Constitution. *Habeas corpus* means "you have the body" in Latin. It describes the right of an individual accused of a crime to appear before a court, where a judge can determine whether the arrest was legal. Lincoln argued that he could suspend it under emergency powers granted by the Constitution, as a way of preventing Confederate sympathizers from disrupting the Union's war mobilization. But Lincoln at one point defied a ruling by the Supreme Court to do so. Similarly, about 80 years later, Franklin D. Roosevelt invoked the emergency powers when he ordered that all Japanese Americans living on the West Coast, many of them native U.S. citizens, be sent to **internment**

camps. The Supreme Court, though divided, upheld that executive order as necessary for national security.

FDR had already struggled with the court over presidential authority early in his second term. Although his programs were popular, the Supreme Court had declared two of them unconstitutional.

Almost 130,000 Japanese Americans sold their homes and businesses to move to the camps.

Roosevelt countered by proposing a bill to Congress that would have given him the power to name as many as six additional judges to the nine-person court. As the bill gained support in Congress and public criticism of the Supreme Court intensified, the court seemed to soften its stance. It allowed more of Roosevelt's

★ If it passes, the president celebrates by signing it in front of the members of Congress who supported it the most. He'll sometimes even sign it using several pens, which then become prized keepsakes. ★

proposals to stand. Eventually, congressional support for Roosevelt's bill to "pack" the Supreme Court dwindled. The president may have lost that battle, but he succeeded in expanding the federal government's role overall.

The most basic power presidents have is in regard to policymaking. Congress still proposes, argues over, and votes on new laws. The president can suggest a new law, too, but someone in the House or the Senate has to sponsor it. Then the congressperson has to convince his or her colleagues to pass it. If it passes,

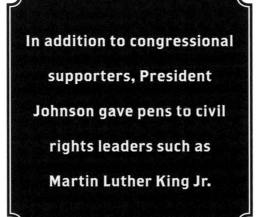

In addition to congressional supporters, President Johnson gave pens to civil rights leaders such as Martin Luther King Jr.

the president celebrates by signing it in front of the members of Congress who supported it the most. He'll sometimes even sign it using several pens, which then become prized keepsakes. (Johnson used more than 75 pens to sign the Civil Rights Act in 1964.) A presidential signing makes the bill a law. If the Supreme Court later decides the law is unconstitutional, it becomes **null**.

Presidents have sometimes issued "signing statements" when they've signed a bill. George W. Bush notably made extensive and controversial use of such

The president has two veto options.

1 A PRESIDENT MAY ACTIVELY VETO A BILL

Congress can then override the veto with the support of two-thirds of the House or Senate (whichever chamber proposed the bill). The other chamber must then also get a two-thirds majority before the bill becomes law.

2 A PRESIDENT MAY NEITHER SIGN NOR VETO

After the next 10 days, if Congress is in session, the bill becomes law anyway. If a congressional session ends before the 10 days is up, the bill is canceled.

UNCOVERING POWERS

proclamations. Bush often criticized parts of bills as unconstitutional or even stated his unwillingness to enforce parts of them. In turn, he was criticized for trying to use such statements as a type of veto.

One of the president's greatest powers comes into play when he *doesn't* sign a bill. *Veto* is Latin for "I forbid." It means the president is preventing a bill Congress has passed from becoming law. A president may actively veto a bill immediately or simply wait for 10 days. After that time, an unsigned bill may be canceled by what's known as a "pocket veto," if Congress is not in session.

A veto is a significant move. If congressional leaders feel strongly enough about the bill, they can try to pass it again. But they need the support of two-thirds of their colleagues to make the proposal a law without the president's signature—a steeper challenge than mustering the simple majority (one vote more than half) needed to get a bill to the president in the first place. This second attempt is called a veto override.

> In his first term, President Obama signed 654 bills into law and vetoed only 2—1 of which was a pocket veto.

18 REPUBLICAN

16 DEMOCRATIC

Eighteen members of the **REPUBLICAN PARTY** and 16 members of the **DEMOCRATIC PARTY** have served as president. Ten presidents have been from older parties or were unaffiliated (George Washington).

NEVER ELECTED

GERALD FORD was the only president never to be elected vice president or president. A representative of Michigan, Ford was named vice president when Spiro Agnew resigned in 1973. Ford became president the next year, thanks to Nixon's resignation.

43

YOUNGEST

JOHN KENNEDY, at age 43, was the youngest to be elected president.

73

OLDEST

RONALD REAGAN, at age 73 (for his second term), was the oldest to be elected president.

CHAPTER 4

THE PATH OF PRESIDENTIAL POWER

THE U.S. PRESIDENCY

Every four years, voters in the U.S. decide whom they want as president. According to the media and the candidates, every election is a critical one. It is a decision that will determine the nation's future course.

Some people disagree. Historian Andrew Bacevich argues in *The Limits of Power* that **interest groups** and official systems work to make sure things stay the same, no matter who is president. And many times in U.S. history, a sitting vice president has sought to succeed his boss, promising to continue the same programs and policies. In times when people have had jobs and were making money, some candidates have been reluctant to propose dramatic changes. How critical could such elections really be?

Presidential elections are often important in ways voters can't see on Election Day. World events can change conditions

★ **Any person elected to the presidency has to be ready for the unexpected. It can define his or her place in history and the presidency itself.** ★

THE PATH OF PRESIDENTIAL POWER

suddenly and dramatically, as they did following the September 11 terror attacks in 2001. They can cast presidents into unexpected crises, often involving other nations. Such situations demand that a president demonstrate a type of leadership quite different from what he uses in proposing laws to Congress, signing bills, or performing traditional duties such as lighting the national Christmas tree. Any person elected to the presidency has to be ready for the unexpected. It can define his or her place in history and the presidency itself.

In a 2008 campaign speech, candidate Obama identified "terrorism and nuclear weapons, climate change and poverty,

genocide and disease" as key international issues a new president would face. Such threats are still present today.

In the meantime, other factors have prompted new ways of viewing presidential powers. Presidents now need to consider how to deal with aggressors—such as terrorist groups—who don't represent any particular nation and have unclear leadership and goals. They must navigate through a thicket of political, environmental, and economic issues centered on energy concerns. They must also exercise **diplomacy** when confronting nations that seem to act in purposely disruptive ways. Indeed, new dilemmas constantly appear. How to protect government secrets—or even have them—in the

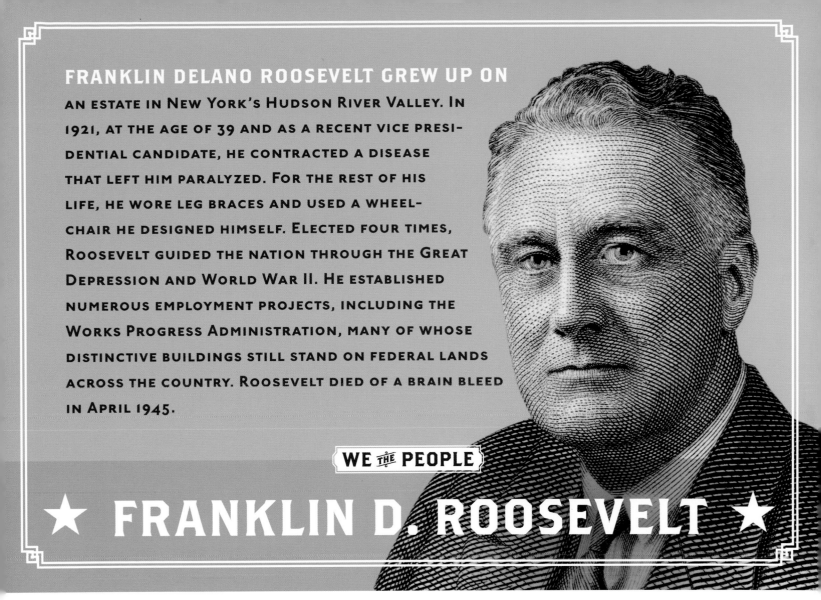

FRANKLIN DELANO ROOSEVELT GREW UP ON AN ESTATE IN NEW YORK'S HUDSON RIVER VALLEY. IN 1921, AT THE AGE OF 39 AND AS A RECENT VICE PRESIDENTIAL CANDIDATE, HE CONTRACTED A DISEASE THAT LEFT HIM PARALYZED. FOR THE REST OF HIS LIFE, HE WORE LEG BRACES AND USED A WHEELCHAIR HE DESIGNED HIMSELF. ELECTED FOUR TIMES, ROOSEVELT GUIDED THE NATION THROUGH THE GREAT DEPRESSION AND WORLD WAR II. HE ESTABLISHED NUMEROUS EMPLOYMENT PROJECTS, INCLUDING THE WORKS PROGRESS ADMINISTRATION, MANY OF WHOSE DISTINCTIVE BUILDINGS STILL STAND ON FEDERAL LANDS ACROSS THE COUNTRY. ROOSEVELT DIED OF A BRAIN BLEED IN APRIL 1945.

WE THE PEOPLE

★ FRANKLIN D. ROOSEVELT ★

age of social media and the Internet? How to command and structure the armed forces when warfare can be waged by remote control?

As has long been the case, future presidents will have to redefine America's role among its international allies—and enemies. American involvement in one conflict after another, from Vietnam in the 1960s and '70s to the War on Terror today, has resulted in both criticism and praise. Sometimes the most negative reactions have come from Americans themselves. President Woodrow Wilson (1913–21), for example, had to overcome significant resistance at home when the U.S. joined World War I. Later, he won the Nobel Peace Prize for his efforts to establish lasting postwar peace.

More recently, President Obama was criticized at home for his calls to respect

BEST REMEMBERED FOR HIS UNCEREMONIOUS EXIT FROM POLITICS, RICHARD NIXON'S START WAS PROMISING. HE WAS A CONGRESSMAN, SENATOR, AND THEN VICE PRESIDENT FOR TWO TERMS UNDER DWIGHT D. EISENHOWER. AFTER LOSING THE 1960 PRESIDENTIAL RACE TO KENNEDY, NIXON RETURNED IN 1968 FOR THE FIRST OF HIS TWO PRESIDENTIAL WINS. HE GUIDED U.S. INVOLVEMENT IN THE VIETNAM WAR TO A CLOSE AND ESTABLISHED THE ENVIRONMENTAL PROTECTION AGENCY. BUT A BURGLARY AT THE DEMOCRATIC NATIONAL COMMITTEE HEADQUARTERS AT WASHINGTON, D.C.'S WATERGATE HOTEL IN JUNE 1972 LED TO REVELATIONS OF WIDESPREAD CRIMINAL ACTIVITY INVOLVING MEMBERS OF NIXON'S ADMINISTRATION. HE RESIGNED IN 1974.

WE ⭐ THE PEOPLE

★ RICHARD NIXON ★

other nations' values and interests. Such tolerance was viewed by some as not supporting a leadership role for the U.S. That role, which includes the military and, usually, an interest in spreading democracy and human rights around the world, is sometimes described by historians and politicians themselves as "American exceptionalism."

Tensions in the Middle East have proven particularly difficult for U.S. presidents to resolve. Those tensions, based on both religion and politics, have existed for centuries. However, when Israel became a nation in 1948, its right to certain territories was disputed. Fighting in the region has been a fact of life ever since. Although U.S. presidents and their secretaries of state have been committed to ending conflict in the region, that goal has been elusive. But the effort is necessary. According to Steven A. Cook and

professor Shibley Telhami, "Failure to forge an agreement will present serious complications for other American policies in the Middle East because the Arab-Israeli conflict remains central not only to Israel and its neighbors but also to the way most Arabs view the United States."

Meanwhile, political strife between the

Jerusalem is claimed as the capital city of both Israel and the State of Palestine.

parties can eat up a president's energies. Sometimes there are ways around it, though.

President Obama, for instance, made frequent use of executive orders and memoranda to bring about change within federal agencies when he was unable to get congressional support.

In 2014, Obama used an executive order

★ Obama also used executive orders several times
to fine-tune laws that made it through Congress—
particularly the 2010 Affordable Care Act. ★

THE PATH OF PRESIDENTIAL POWER

to protect from deportation millions of U.S. workers who were in the country illegally. He did this basically by declining to enforce parts of existing immigration law. Later that year, Obama restored diplomatic ties with Cuba through executive action. (A 1962 executive order by Kennedy was what had first restricted trade and travel to Cuba.) Obama ordered secretary of state John Kerry to re-establish a relationship with Cuba and to reopen the U.S. embassy in Havana. He also ordered that long-standing restrictions on travel to Cuba be eased.

Cuban tourism, once promoted in the 1950s, may soon be revived, thanks to a December 2014 executive order.

Obama also used executive orders several times to fine-tune laws that made it through Congress—particularly the 2010 Affordable Care Act. His executive actions brought loud objections from Republicans. They said he was abusing power not granted by the Constitution. House Republicans even passed a bill outlining a way for Congress to sue the president if he used executive orders to get around any laws. According to House Majority Leader Eric Cantor, "The president's dangerous search for expanded powers appears to be endless."

CONSTITUTIONAL POWERS

THOSE STATED DIRECTLY IN THE CONSTITUTION

DELEGATED POWERS

THOSE GRANTED TO THE PRESIDENT BY CONGRESS

TYPES OF PRESIDENTIAL POWER

INHERENT POWERS

THOSE ESSENTIAL TO THE PRESIDENT'S ROLE AS HEAD OF THE EXECUTIVE BRANCH

EMERGENCY POWERS are enacted during crises such as wars or natural disasters. These powers include providing federal assistance to declared disaster areas, deploying military personnel, and suspending certain rights and freedoms.

EXECUTIVE ORDERS are official rules signed and issued by the president that carry the weight of laws but do not require congressional approval. The orders are most often used to tell federal agencies how to enact and enforce laws and procedures.

EXECUTIVE PRIVILEGE is the right of the president and executive officials to withhold information from the public at their discretion. Primarily used to protect diplomatic secrets or military procedures, executive privilege also allows the president to withhold certain information from the legislative and judicial branches.

THE PATH OF PRESIDENTIAL POWER

Although the executive order has been a tool favored by nearly all presidents faced with an uncooperative or slow Congress, scholars were divided. University of Chicago Law School professor Eric Posner said Obama's use of executive orders was "just routine stuff" with plenty of precedent. But Michael W. McConnell, a Stanford University law professor and former federal judge, said that Obama reached beyond his authority with his executive order on immigration enforcement. "Of all the stretches of executive power Americans have seen in the past few years, the president's unilateral suspension of statutes may have the most disturbing long-term effects," he said.

Other issues may not demand new uses

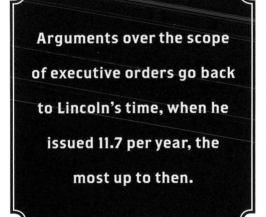

Arguments over the scope of executive orders go back to Lincoln's time, when he issued 11.7 per year, the most up to then.

of presidential power, but they will challenge the president's reading of the voters' wishes. One issue emerging as the 2016 presidential campaign got underway was the growing concentration of wealth among the already wealthy. Another was the dramatically increasing cost of a college education.

The distribution of power among the three branches of government, particularly between Congress and the president, will undoubtedly continue to swing. But there's little question that when Americans look for a decision, for a message to other nations, or even for a way to think about a tragedy, they will look to the president—the voice of the entire nation.

amendment   a change, clarification, or addition to the U.S. Constitution, proposed by Congress and approved by three-fourths of the states

bribery   paying for favors that are illegal or not available to others

cabinet   a group of people appointed by a head of a government to lead executive departments and serve as advisers

censured   received a formal expression of extreme disapproval

constitutionality   the status of a law in relation to the powers and principles spelled out in the Constitution

diplomacy   discussion or negotiations between nations

impeachment   a process of bringing formal charges against a government official for crimes committed while in office

interest groups   people organized to try to create or preserve laws that favor specific causes, industries, or activities, such as gun rights, energy production, or free speech

internment   detention or confinement

intrigue   plots or strategies by enemies to trick each other, or destroy one another's plans or work

null   invalid or no longer legal

precedent   an action or decision that justifies or serves as the model for later actions or decisions

presidential succession   the order in which top governmental officials are placed in the event that the president dies while in office, resigns, or is otherwise unable to perform the job

radical   thorough or drastic, or favoring thorough or drastic political change

stalemate   a deadlock or standstill

subsidies   funds paid by a government to an individual, business, or industry, usually to aid growth or as protection from price swings

tariffs   charges, or a kind of tax, on certain imported and exported goods

treason   an attempt to overthrow one's government or help its enemies

veto   a cancellation by an executive of a measure approved by others

SELECTED BIBLIOGRAPHY

Atlas, James, ed. *How They See Us: Meditations on America*. New York: Atlas & Co., 2010. Distributed by W. W. Norton.

Bacevich, Andrew J. *The Limits of Power: The End of American Exceptionalism*. New York: Metropolitan Books, 2008.

Davis, Todd, and Marc Frey. *The New Big Book of U.S. Presidents*. Philadelphia: Running Press Kids, 2013.

Fisher, Louis. *Presidential War Power*. 3rd ed. Lawrence: University Press of Kansas, 2013.

Haass, Richard N., Martin Indyk, and the Brookings Saban Center. *Restoring the Balance: A Middle East Strategy for the Next President*. Washington, D.C.: Brookings Institution Press, 2008.

Lifton, Robert Jay. *Superpower Syndrome: America's Apocalyptic Confrontation with the World*. New York: Nation Books, 2003.

Rubel, David. *Scholastic Encyclopedia of the Presidents and Their Times*. New York: Scholastic, 1994.

Woods, Thomas E. *The Politically Incorrect Guide to American History*. Washington, D.C.: Regnery, 2004.

WEBSITES

American Government

www.ushistory.org/gov/7a.asp

Review how the modern presidency was defined, and check out Article II for yourself.

Smithsonian: The American Presidency

americanhistory.si.edu/presidency/home.html

Learn more about the people, campaigns, and ideas that have shaped the presidency.

Note: Every effort has been made to ensure that the websites listed above are suitable for children, that they have educational value, and that they contain no inappropriate material. However, because of the nature of the Internet, it is impossible to guarantee that these sites will remain active indefinitely or that their contents will not be altered.

Published by **Creative Education** and **Creative Paperbacks**
P.O. Box 227, Mankato, Minnesota 56002
Creative Education and Creative Paperbacks are imprints of **The Creative Company**
www.thecreativecompany.us

Design and production by **Christine Vanderbeek**
Art direction by **Rita Marshall**
Printed in China

Photographs by Alamy (Everett Collection Inc.), Corbis (AP, Bettmann, Christy Bowe, Dennis Brack/CNP/AdMedia, Christie's Images, CORBIS, David J. Frent/David J. & Janice L. Frent Collection, Bob Gomel/Sygma, K.J. Historical, Wally McNamee, David Pollack, Joseph Sohm/Visions of America),

Creative Commons Wikimedia (Eliphalet Frazer Andrews/The White House Historical Association, Baker Art Gallery, Mathew Brady/U.S. National Archives and Records Administration, The Bureau of Engraving and Printing, Ralph Eleaser Whiteside Earl/The White House, Alexander Gardner/Library of Congress, Frederick Kemmelmeyer/Metropolitan Museum of Art, Bob McNeely/U.S. Federal Government, National Portrait Gallery, The Obama-Biden Transition Project, Pach Brothers/Library of Congress, Rembrandt Peale/The White House Historical Association, Frank O. Salisbury/The White House Historical Association, Gilbert Stuart, U.S. Federal Government, U.S. National Archives and Records

Administration), Getty Images (Nicholas Kamm), Shutterstock (Steve Heap, Kapreski, lkeskinen, Sean Pavone)

Library of Congress Cataloging-in-Publication Data
McAuliffe, Bill.
The U.S. Presidency / Bill McAuliffe.
p. cm. — (By the people)
Includes bibliographical references and index.
Summary: A historical survey of the United States presidency, from its beginnings to current issues, including its role as executive and influential presidents such as Andrew Jackson.

ISBN 978-1-60818-676-1 *(hardcover)*
ISBN 978-1-62832-272-9 *(pbk)*
ISBN 978-1-56660-712-4 *(eBook)*
1. Presidents—United States—Juvenile literature.

JK517.M329 2016
973.09/9—dc23   2015039276

CCSS: RI.5.1, 2, 3, 8; RI. 6.1, 2, 4, 7; RH.6-8.3, 4, 5, 6, 7, 8

First Edition HC 9 8 7 6 5 4 3 2 1
First Edition PBK 9 8 7 6 5 4 3 2 1

Pictured on cover: George Washington